Social Justice Sundries

Poems by Contessa Sanchez

Social Justice Sundries

Contact the author at:

Contessasanchez@gmail.com

Dedicated to everyone to whom these poems represent.

Contents

Compliant Unrest..(

Unmanned Drones...7

Sexism...

Anonymous to Free Speech..9

Mental Health..10

People of Color in the Movie Industry...............................1

Sex Work...1

Modern Living>Environment..14

Political Frustrations..1

Revolution on Canvas...1

Unlock Wedlock...1

What are You?...1

2008-Present Trauma..2

Freedom?..23

M2F..2

Racial Discourse..2

Domestic Violence Blame...2(

Being an Ally...28

Guantanamo...2

Ms. and Ms. in Love..3(

Male Domestic Abuse..3

21st Century Slave...3

No Religion?..3

Ferguson..35

Sex Positive..36

Mexican't...38

"Freedom of Speech"..39

Rape Recovery...40

Bootleg American..41

Bisexual...42

Compliant Unrest

I was barely a child
when the Rwanda Genocide
struck a country
as a teenager
I pondered how such
a thing could happen
and how the rest
of the world could seem
so silent
as an adult
I watched uprisings
on the news
with protests and violent attacks
saw images saturated
with the unrest
refugee numbers and
civil wars rise
and too much of the world was silent
compliant
it seems to happen
every time

Unmanned Drones

Unmanned Drones
Armed with missiles and bombs
Overhead predators
Cheaper and remotely flown
Target killing Drones
In and outside combat zones
Covert
Making it impossible to know
How many civilians became casualties
A departed, dead unknown
Improving tactics
So fewer men on a side should die
The art of war
High tech with "bug splat"
A video game of war

Sexism

The safe bounds of childhood home life served as an
idealistic, innocent time.
Where eyes were blind
Creating no gender based crimes
Where mistakes stood corrected and achievements held high.
This morality taught that gender played no games
Time plus dedication was all one could ever need
It was a story book life deserted to the non-fiction realm with
the unjust distinctions
Of a woman in a man's world.
From the conditions I've seen, a body serves to determine
self-worth, never mind the range of
Attitudes and individuality.
It all comes down to body parts
That's what sexism taught me.

Anonymous to Free Speech

I will teach you not to ask for the sake
of the existing state.
In order to remain safe
I will teach you not to question, to willingly comply,
listen to another's request, rule, or political wish
even though you deserve an outcry.
We must tread with carefully lined lips,
wary of the growing wound of politics.
There was a time where my generation could willfully speak
its mind
but freedom of speech is a fading dream
or perhaps we were just naïve
or easily deceived.
Now who will be injured for taking a stand,
kept from proceeding,
no longer leading?
We voted with our dollar bills
but had to trade in our ideals
and look where terror brought us,
much worse than a political standstill.
My dream was to raise a child where expression could roam
free with their creativity
not deterrence or detainment run by unfair policies.
At first we gave little attention
but now there's the fear to convey your convictions
at various demonstrations.
So in order to remain safe I will teach you not to question,
to willingly comply,
listen to another's request, rule, or political wish
even though you deserve an outcry.

Mental Health

Schizophrenic
On the bus
Hearing sounds and conversations
Which sanctions
A newspaper hat for self-preservation
Calling out to prevent imagined vocalization
Diverting into a mental health isolation
Disillusioned by the splitting mind

Passengers
Stay warily behind
Thinking up terms like crazed or nutty
While the whole time
They don't think it's funny
But when symptoms were vague
They dismissed what was easily missed

Made up despair
A blue heavy heart
Uncomfortable fear

Symptoms of the feeble
Picturing phases that will eventually clear
Because the physical condition is what matters
Not what rests upstairs
But no
That way they speak just can't be
Problems dreamed up by the faint of heart
Please

An over-reaction
Is what they wanted to see
Like you can just wash it away
As if cancer was an annoyance
You could just wish away
Yet on any given day
It should be all health that matters

So let's end the shame
For what's mentally strange
And change it to acceptance
There's those wanting aid
Who shouldn't be carried away
By the untrained who blame
Or claim there's no issues to handle

It's easy to deal with a cast
Or something that shattered fast
But when someone hears voices
Or downed by depression
Or anxiety tension
Or fill in the blank characterization
They should know there's someone there to listen

People of Color in the Movie Industry

Going to the movies I look at actors who
always stand apart from me. Yet my wish
is to look at the mainstream movie screen and
see more people with my color scheme.
That purge away stereotypes that usually come
up with POC.

In unwavering defense, I hear it's the director's art.
But how many white men do we need to play
nonwhite ethnic parts?

Mainstream media,
do not attempt to play this off.
Quoting the one African, Asian, Mexican-American
in your film before they're killed off.

Keep your token characters
we deserve an equal part.
With the hope that it won't take
a whole generation to show less racism or exclusion
in motion picture art.

Sex Work

Judging my sex work occupation

Thinking I'm unintelligent and a whore

Standards you claim

As you tune in for triple X porn

I feel I've come to realize
that our standards impede a more sustainable way that grows
free from finite living.
There's a shortage of resources that we standardly cling to
and are too comfortable to say goodbye to.
Thus living greener is a half held endeavor while depleting
the earth of non-renewable pleasures.
We lure stress to this sphere's existence because we're barely
working toward coexistence.
Thriving on the exploitation, creating damage for the next
generation
instead we should focus on adaptation.
But alas, our standards cling to the mess of the go green
insuccess no matter how harmful the effects.

Political Frustrations

People ask for dialogues
and meetings for resolutions agreed
upon on paper.
But change is just a wish
if it only acts in words.

Revolution on Canvas

My university is a revolution on canvas.
Its knowledge shared in academic papers that rarely spread
to the accessibility of the internet or non-student.

But academia is not without merit.
It researches and lectures on subjects from
political science to human anatomy.
And let's not forget the combination for degrees and
certificates.

The information is there but while standing on campus
I see an institution that has so much to offer
besides paper diplomas.

Information can change the world
yet my school seems more focused on tuition payments
and donations changing hands.

Education should be accessible and offered to anyone
willing to take the time to nourish their mind.
So that anyone can read or listen to lectures that might
help them advance in life.

To claim to have the latest technology, breakthrough
advancements, and curricula meant to mold minds should be
a specialization in its diversity.

Not in the complications of who, through out of pocket
payments or mounting debt can, for a moment, have access.

Higher education should be a revolution for how it transforms any population to be more than they were before. Yet a revolution on canvas is what I see, walking across this campus like so many other educational run business strategies.

Unlock Wedlock

I don't need to sign a piece of paper to let you know I love
you.
For what commitment lies in a signature that my lips haven'
already told you?
For a group of people to hear an exclamation of "I do" has n
bearing on any thoughts I have toward you.
A celebration of love they say?
Well, we celebrate every day.
And I don't need a white wedding dress to represent a
walking debt
even if it's financed.
Just like we don't need wrapped boxes of toasters and plates
to say "congrats, what a special date."
Yet weddings seem to be all the rage
despite the fact they're on a political stage.
But I don't need to sign a piece of paper to let you know I
love you.
For what commitment lies in a signature that my lips haven'
already told you?

What are You?

Being stared at with preconceptions
is never quite the same
day by day

My hoop earrings "too ghetto"
my accent "too white"

Mislabeled or misread
"But what are you?"
constantly asked instead

Representing me there's no one nation
but either my halves will be
used to condemn me

My birth country too prideful
to do anything but "other" me
we're globalized but change takes
more time

Asked if I'm illegal because I reside
near the borderline
or recalling conversations
talked at
informed my shade is kinda light
so I must be white

Then next week asked to translate
because clearly I'm bilingual

I wish the side eye, double takes, and frown forming
preconceptions would disappear
especially when my ethnicity
is used to direct poor social cues

Made to a covertly formed racialized thought
process that constantly changes when
someone finds a new box they think
I'd fit best in

2008-Present Trauma

Before I said goodbye
everyone I met knew me as
the girl who lied.

People like friends
acting like strangers
down any and all sidewalks or classrooms
like I was some piece of poor taste theater.

But what if I were gone?
There was no self respect in
anything they claimed I'd done.

But I wasn't ready for any of that.
I became lost in the campus
where we first met.

You scared me and soon I became undone.

Threats to my safety
reminded to cease, shut up, forget about
that rape story...

I never knew 16 could be so hard.
I was just too trusting and some
people you perceive as friends can
be cruelly lusting.

I know I'll never forget that night
or what it's like to never hear
"I believe you" from a single person
in your sight. Now I just see a damaged
girl, a part of me still suffering at 16.

I thought I could be stronger
but truly, some things will never get better.

Freedom?

In a country that declares
freedom for others
while holding liberty hostage
in their authority of land
creates the need for
caution as citizens question
the representation of their flag

M2F

I would never want my child to feel trapped based off of born biology.
So when she said she could never be a man I took her seriously.
Growing up, I bought her skirts and plastic dress up beads.
She said she couldn't wait to get her first pair of real earrings.
I did all of this because I respect her whole being
And that she can be whoever she wants to be.
Her happiness is all that should matter,
I rejoiced the day I got to meet my daughter.

Racial Discourse

Racial discourses

filled in white supremacy

show stupidity

among those who deem

themselves worthy of

soap boxes

Domestic Violence Blame

Sitting with a black eye and a cut lip my mother says,

"Wouldn't it have all ended better if you hadn't hit back?"

Staring down at my injured fist I ponder the meaning of

domestic abuse and what it means to be a victim.

Yes, I did strike back.

I was done waiting for the better,

for the improved, nonviolent parallel that never came.

For the partner that now just acted out rage.

And I'm asked why I chose to self protect

Apparently society teaches that good

battered women are the ones who never fight back.

The fist time someone saw the bruising they asked, "what did

I say?"

Because even then somehow I was to blame.

And then there were the neighbors' whispers of, "why does

she stay?"

Because I was trapped in the honeymoon stage,

that this time he'd change, thinking that everything would

become okay.

But if my time with exploited love has taught me anything,

it's that not all victims are the same, that not all victims act

the same.

That we are not fools or idiots but sometimes stuck on repeat.

But we could do without the blame.

The blame that comes so quickly from those who have

never had to lie about where they got a black eye.

The blame is the abuser's

every time.

Being an Ally

There is nothing wrong with having passion
just the must need for understanding
that every struggle might not be deemed
relatable to your own

you must be the caring outsider
who listens and than speaks
not the one who claims we are all
just one human race
while concurrently placing your stance
above those who've experienced life
as you never have

there is nothing wrong with craving equality,
being an ally, activist, or fighting for a cause

but there will always be an issue
when you speak for and not with

Guantanamo

Guantanamo
How could such a place exist?
That black hole of untimed despair
Run by my people — American people.
How could one really say it's fair?
Have the days passed where humanity was in the air?

The people in power share the news to
Not me — not you — not he or she
Yet we know it's there, that black hole is a shroud we all wear.
When is torture unfit for news?
When our flag soaks up blood we all untune.

What barrier bounds us from crying out dignity, a loss of heart or gain of cruelty?
Why do I not hear enough of "I care!"
You see we have a voice it's one to share.

Could a mine field of intolerance ever call out peace or justice?
We're criminals for keeping silent
Uncharged men just disappear.
Just think, how long could you survive it?

How long could you take the solitary confinement which is your tomb,
Walls that close in, and confiscated time that ticks away
As the days blur into the blank canvas of what was once life.

How could one really say it's fair, being trapped in a black hole of untimed despair?
We all know it's there
So perhaps...there really is no more humanity in the air.

29

Ms. and Ms. in Love

Can I love as you love?
I can love as you love.

I have an attractive frame, an open mind,
And hands that can feel and touch and grasp
Just as your hands can.

My partner is a soul mate wrapped up in love.
She doesn't mind matching anatomy.
Like she doesn't mind curious bi-standards,
Straight he to she interlocks, or question-marked inklings.

We share a passion, a flirt, and friendship built to loving
mates.
We share nights made up with constant laughter,
Mornings with snoozed alarm clocks.

We call it a relationship
Others call it mistakes.

Yet I can love as you love
So instead I'll always say,

Let love be free, unconfined to strict, unrelenting lines.
How could love be love otherwise?

Male Domestic Abuse

There's a domestic abuse ban
Hiding a world where there's any injured man.
It's a ban because what man would ever let a woman lay a
hand?

Antagonistic epidemic
Horrible double standard, one that ensues every blunder.

You are firm
You are strong
You are bold

Any less brings shame to that gender's strong hold.
Who to tell, what to say when everyone underestimates?

Humiliating stigma
A black mark of blame

Shoved and pushed and verbally burnt yet no one came
For what is a man if he's suffered this way?
If he falls victim to her angry shouts?

Any form of violence undefeated by the power of his gender
equates to a domestic abuse blunder.

But what threat could a woman pose?

Exploitation, injustice, fault
Not some misuse of affection or love

Corrupted partnership in no way okay, stands at fault with the
person who causes the pain.

No matter how he's put down

Be it name calling or insults

Hits, kicks, or slaps
Threats or sexually forced acts

Domestic abuse affects all genders

So call an end to this downward double standard.

21st Century Slave

With the invisible chains of ownership you held down my
spirit.
Tried to cripple me like a lame bird and twist my being in
such a way that I forgot that I could feel anything but heavy
exhaustion.
I forgot I could be angry,
I forgot I had rights until my uprising,
because my spirit and being are mine.
In childhood you called me cheap labor, traded like an object
and tricked into slavery.
I remember those locked doors as if they were nightly
bedtime stories and the slaps to my skin like frequent kisses I
wish my mother had been able to give.
It wasn't an upbringing meant for any child,
but you swore up and down your goodness to any stranger
who questioned your morals,
a generous favor.
My thank you is in the form of scar tissue that you left
behind on innocent skin.
Which grew into resentment that told a better story then my
mouth once did.
13 years and a raid it took to remember what kindness was
after a lifetime lost working, mending, fixing, cleaning,
cooking for the selfless you.

I found freedom.

No Religion?

Imagining a world without religion
Would still serve the human condition
Delivering war, oppression, violence, and poverty
Igniting the negative aspects of our society
Incredibly, anything classified or within a system
Can create the belief in controlling traditionalism
If not religion then yes something else
It just happened to take the stand
Because people need belief in something they can
comprehend

Ferguson

Red pavement
spilled from life
taken yet again.

Youth
shot down
racism winning
yet again.

Protect and serve
are only words

when the unarmed
are killed and vilified
for a murder that was
their own.

Sex Positive

Flirtatious funk
That's where I'm told I stand
'Cuz obviously my freedom of body expression is a state of
severe depression.

Sex debate

Telling me how I ought to be, ought to act, ought to see
All for the acceptance of a rude society.

Yet I've got self-respect
You just won't perceive

My body
My life
And how I celebrate it is key.

Sexually positive

Not some cunt, bitch, skank, or hoe

Society, why must you slut slam and shame me?

My body is a beautiful thing and it's my choice to show my
skin or make love to multiple souls,
It's freeing.
It's freeing because I act for me not for a lack of self-esteem.

Yet I see no severe moral dilemma for my counterpart's
naked chest, nor for his constant conquest for my gender's
form, under dressed.

So why do these tables turn so quickly?

Society, we've got quite the mess and it's a conflicting issue at its best.

Mexican't

We were the kind of Mexicans who spoke no Spanish
Raised by people who used no accents
But we treasured the title from a country where we've never lived
And stood as outsiders
Looking in on a culture like foreigners
Yet we studied life to belong
Learned all we could from various books and copied phrases from library glossary pages
But no matter how off-white we stood, Spanish was not our mother tongue
Soon the desire to belong came undone
Despite our wishes
There were only so many times we could mime and use chili in our dishes
Mothers placed hooped earrings in our hands but
Because it hurt to be a tourist in a place we had wished was our land
We chose to disband
And lost half the culture we tried so hard to understand

"Freedom of Speech"

"Freedom of speech"

used so consistently

to infringe on others'

sense of safety and well being

isn't freedom of speech

but a facade

to gain an all-access pass

to being an ass

Rape Recovery

Rape recovery
It is a twisted thing in ways

With flashbacks or not
Either way reminders and thoughts

Self-blame at times or all the time
It's never the same line

Except when it replays and replays in the mind

Rape recovery
It is a twisted thing in ways

But at some point the hope is that the memories fade
Was not your fault is the message to reach

Rape recovery

As you regain the strength to step away from any self-hurt
That you thought would promise comfort but was always
worse

Looking in the mirror and seeing strength in two eyes
Letting die any insult that climbed to your mind

You are beautiful
Not some prize that was demised

You all are beautiful
So just take your time

Don't let anyone tell you otherwise

Bootleg American

English and Spanish interwoven in him
Both a part of him
One brings an ancestry of culture
The other
A place more than just residence
Issues of acceptance balanced on a border lined wall
Where his nationality becomes an agent that will depict his
fall
Never choosing to break any law
He crossed a nation before he knew the reasoning of a wall
Bootleg American
In violation of proper migration
With Spanish and English interwoven in him
Both stand with him
But now he hears half will be the deported end of him

A dim light to follow when this land was all his parents
chased
And now he's displaced
Between the American system that constructed his accent
And some direction on his perspectives
Or a spot on the map with composed traditions
Should he stay?
Will he belong?
Is what he questions as he realizes his parents' land is not a
hundred percent his own
And that America doesn't want to be his home

Bisexual

Some people hint that I've got it best of both ways
Because surely I'm having sex most days
Since I quote, "swing both ways"
But my sexuality isn't a winning hand
When we have straight cis men ruling the land
And there mainstream society stands,
Dictating the parts of me I apparently don't understand
Because you're either gay or straight
Which makes me twisted and kinky
A non-serious part-time lover
Endangering a movement and homophile endeavors
But either way, I find no sin to like it two ways
But no matter what I say I get hate from both ways
Too confused from the gays and outed by the straights
And everyone else has got something else to hate
But how far off could I be on a blurred lined spectrum
That the possibility of bisexual love stands in question?

Acknowledgments

Thank you to the teacher who introduced me to slam poetry.

To Rachel Steinberg, for her constructive criticism and encouragement.

To Nicole McCraw, for sharing a passion in art and feminism.

And to everyone else who supported me while I tried to get my thoughts onto paper.

25425264R00030

Made in the USA
Middletown, DE
03 November 2015